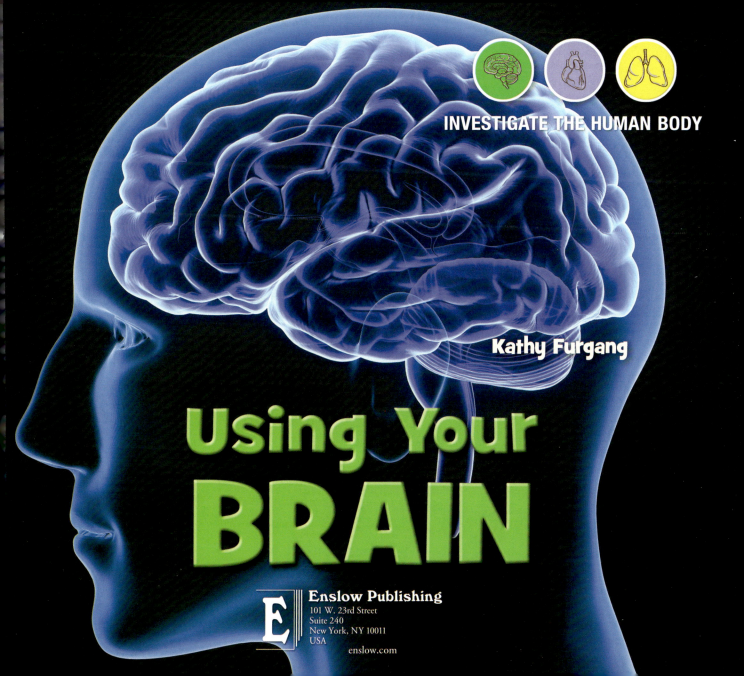

INVESTIGATE THE HUMAN BODY

Kathy Furgang

Using Your BRAIN

Enslow Publishing
101 W. 23rd Street
Suite 240
New York, NY 10011
USA

enslow.com

Words to Know

brain stem A part of the brain that connects the brain to the spinal cord. It controls body movements and messages to and from the body.

cerebellum A part of the brain that controls muscles and balance.

cerebrum The largest part of the brain. It is used to control movements and thoughts.

fiber A thin structure shaped like a thread.

nerve cells Bundles of fibers in the body that send and receive messages.

nervous system The body's system of nerve fibers that travel around the body to control movement.

pituitary gland The part of the brain that controls growth.

process To take in and organize.

spinal cord A bundle of nerve fibers that move along the inside of the spine.

••• Contents

Words to Know 2

How We Use the Brain 4

Parts of the Brain 8

The Brain and
   Nervous System 14

Treat Your Brain Right 18

Activity:
   Keep a Brain Checklist 22

Learn More 24

Index 24

How We Use the Brain

● ● ● Your brain helps you do more than just study for a test. Every time you think, speak, walk, or move a muscle, you are using your brain. Your brain even controls when you blink, swallow, or laugh. The brain is like the command center of the body.

Different parts of the brain do different jobs. Some parts control speech. Others send and receive information about vision or emotions. Your brain sends and receives messages from every part of your body.

Think about it! Your brain controls everything your body does.

Big Brain

By the time you are an adult, your brain will weigh about 3 pounds (1.5 kilograms).

Your brain is at work whether you're taking a test or taking a ride on your skateboard.

Memories include how to do basic tasks like making breakfast.

The Brain and Memories

Your brain works even when you are asleep. You do so much during one day that your brain needs time to **process** and store the information. A lot of this work is done while you are resting or sleeping.

The brain also helps store memories. The brain holds memories about things you did in the past. This includes memories about fun or sad times. But the brain must also store memories about how to do things such as ride a bike, write your name, or use the toaster.

Parts of the Brain

● ● ● In a single day, you may use all parts of your brain. Each part has a different job. The **cerebrum** is the largest part of the brain. It takes up more than 80 percent of the brain's size.

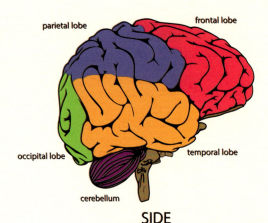
SIDE

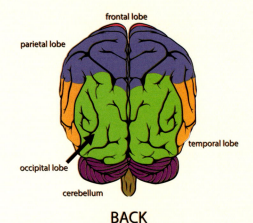
BACK

The brain has a right side and a left side. Each side of the brain is divided into four sections, or lobes.

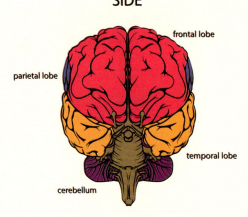
FRONT

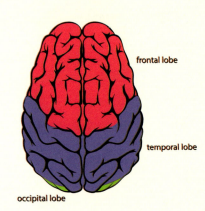
TOP

Bright Idea
You could light up a small lightbulb with the electricity created by your brain activity.

Cerebrum

The cerebrum is divided down the center into two halves, or sides. You use the left side of your brain for tasks that involve logic and analysis. This includes activities like doing math or studying for a test. You use the right side of your brain for tasks that involve creativity or emotion. This includes making art, writing, or singing.

Each side of the brain is then divided into four parts, or lobes. Messages about taste, touch, emotion, memory, and movement are processed in these lobes.

Imagine all of the nerve cells needed for all of the activities people are doing in this play area.

Nerves Cells on the Move

How does the brain handle all the messages from the many parts of the cerebrum? The messages the brain sends and receives are chemical messages. They travel along tiny bundles of **fibers** called **nerve cells**, or neurons.

Each nerve cell in your body is a complex system of connections to other nerve cells. Nerve cells can even change by shrinking, growing, or changing shape. Each change depends on the chemical messages it is sending and receiving.

Sending Signals
The human brain has about 86 billion nerve cells. Each one can carry around 500 signals per second.

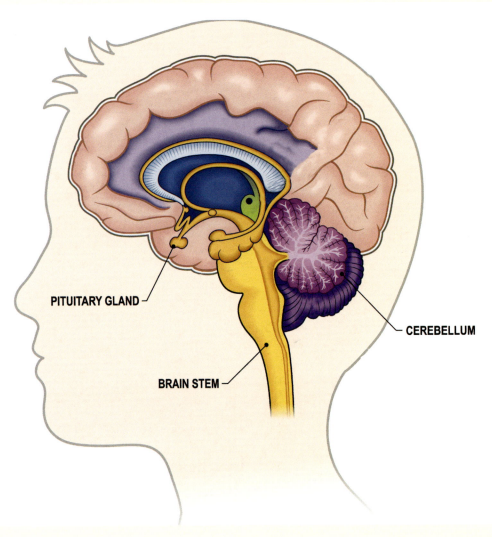

Small parts of the brain also control sleep, alertness, and body temperature.

Help for the Cerebrum

The human brain is so complex that the cerebrum needs some help processing it all! Smaller parts of the brain help sort out the chemical messages of nerve cells.

The **cerebellum** is a small section in the back of the brain. It helps control all of your movements, including ones you don't think much about.

Just beneath the cerebellum is the **brain stem**. It connects the brain to the rest of the body. This part of the brain controls the body functions you don't need to think about at all. These include breathing, digesting food, and the actions of your heart and lungs.

The **pituitary gland** is a tiny, pea-sized part of your brain. It controls growth.

The Brain and Nervous System

The brain is part of a complex system in your body called the **nervous system**. The brain processes the messages that move up and down the brain stem and **spinal cord**. The spinal cord is a big bundle of nerve fibers that move along the inside of your spine. From there, the messages travel throughout all parts of the body. Think of the brain and nervous system as a computer that operates every other part of your body.

The nervous system is protected by bone. The skull protects the brain and the backbone protects the spinal cord.

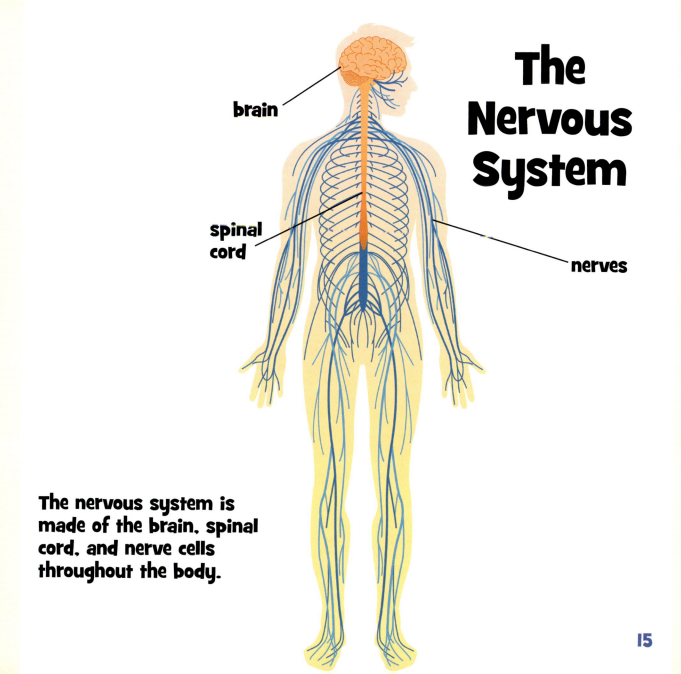

The Nervous System

brain

spinal cord

nerves

The nervous system is made of the brain, spinal cord, and nerve cells throughout the body.

The brain processes the smell, taste, and feel of food and drinks.

A Lot of Nerves

If you stretch out the nerve cells in an adult's nervous system, they would stretch 37 miles (60 kilometers).

The Nervous System at Work

The nervous system works by sending nerve cell signals that control every muscle in your body. Some muscle movements, such as running or jumping, take effort. Others happen without you even thinking about them. Whenever your heart beats or you swallow food, you are moving muscles controlled by the nervous system.

The nervous system also controls the senses. Everything you see, taste, smell, hear, or touch is the result of messages to and from the brain and nervous system. The eyes, tongue, nose, ears, and skin have special nerve cells that communicate with the brain about everything you see and do.

Treat Your Brain Right

The brain is one of the body's most amazing organs. That's why it's important to take care of it. Sleep is one of the most important ways to take care of your brain. Young people need more sleep than adults. A young person's brain is still growing. While you sleep, the brain has a chance to rest from all the activity it has been part of throughout the day.

Exercise Your Brain

The brain needs care and attention, just like any other part of the body. Exercise is a great way to keep the brain strong and healthy. Activities like running, biking, or playing sports build muscles and coordination. This keeps the brain working.

In addition to helping the brain, sleep also helps keep you from getting sick.

Exercise makes the brain strong!

Go to Bed!

Doctors say that children between the ages of 6 and 13 should get between 9 and 11 hours of sleep every night. How long do you sleep each night?

But studying, reading, and doing homework also exercise the brain in important ways. Puzzles and word searches help build brain power and make connections between nerve cells. Even talking to other people can use lots of nerve cells throughout your body. All of these nerve cells are controlled by your body's own supercomputer—the brain!

Activity: Keep a Brain Checklist

● ● ● Keep track of your brain-healthy activities for three days.

1. For three days, write about the activities you do that are good for your brain. Think about how many hours of sleep you get and the activities you do for your body and mind.
2. Write about how you feel after each activity. How can you improve the activities you do to make your brain healthy and strong?
3. Try to make one or more of the changes you came up with. Then keep track of your brain-healthy activities for the next three days. Were you able to get more sleep? Did you exercise, read, or play more games that require thinking? Talk or write about the changes you made.

Brain Checklist

	Hours of Sleep	Physical Activity	Brain Activity
DAY 1			
DAY 2			
DAY 3			

Learn More

Books

Bozzo, Linda. *Brain and Behavior*. Vero Beach, FL: Rourke Educational Media, 2018.

DK. *Human Body!* New York, NY: DK Publishing, 2017.

Drimmer, Stephanie Warren. *Brain Games: Big Book of Boredom Busters.* Washington, DC.: National Geographic Children's Books, 2018.

Websites

DK Find Out!
www.dkfindout.com/uk/human-body/
Visit an interactive website all about the human body. Learn more about the nervous system or any other topic related to the body.

Kids Health
kidshealth.org/en/kids/?WT.ac=p2k
Play games and take quizzes about health and the human body.

Index

bone 14
brain stem 13, 14
cerebellum 13
cerebrum 8, 9, 11, 13
creativity 9
emotions 4, 9
exercise 18, 21, 22
lobes 9
logic 9
memory 7, 9
nerve cells 11, 13, 17, 18, 21
nervous system 14, 17
pituitary gland 13
senses 17
sleep 7, 18, 21, 22
spinal cord 14
vision 4

Published in 2020 by Enslow Publishing, LLC
101 W. 23rd Street, Suite 240, New York, NY 10011

Copyright © 2020 by Enslow Publishing, LLC.
All rights reserved.

No part of this book may be reproduced by any means without the written permission of the publisher.

Library of Congress Cataloging-in-Publication Data
Names: Furgang, Kathy, author.
Title: Using your brain / Kathy Furgang.
Description: New York : Enslow Publishing, 2020. | Series: Investigate the human body | Audience: Grade K-4 | Includes bibliographical references and index.
Identifiers: LCCN 2019013429| ISBN 9781978512917 (library bound) | ISBN 9781978512894 (paperback) | ISBN 9781978512900 (6 pack)
Subjects: LCSH: Brain--Juvenile literature. | Nervous system--Juvenile literature.
Classification: LCC QP376 .F87 2020 | DDC 612.8/2--dc23
LC record available at https://lccn.loc.gov/2019013429

Printed in the United States of America

To Our Readers: We have done our best to make sure all website addresses in this book were active and appropriate when we went to press. However, the author and the publisher have no control over and assume no liability for the material available on those websites or on any websites they may link to. Any comments or suggestions can be sent by email to customerservice@enslow.com.

Photos Credits: Using Your Brain – Research by Bruce Donnola

Cover, p. 1 Life science/Shutterstock.com; pp. 3, 5 Jacek Chabraszewski/Shutterstock.com; pp. 3, 6 Phovoir/Shutterstock.com; pp. 3, 15 normaals/iStock/Getty Images; pp. 3, 19 New Africa/Shutterstock.com; pp. 3, 6 Always_Sunshine/Shutterstock.com; p. 7 AT Production/Shutterstock.com; p. 8 Christos Georghiou/Shutterstock.com; p. 10 Svetlana123/Shutterstock.com; p. 12 jambojam/iStock/Getty Images; p. 16 PR Image Factory/Shutterstock.com; p. 20 Sergey Novikov/Shutterstock.com; p. 23 YanLev/Shutterstock.com; cover graphics blackpencil/Shutterstock.com